The Wrong Shade
of Red

Camilla Paaske Christensen

BookLeaf
Publishing

India | USA | UK

Presentation by *BookLeaf Publishing*

Web: www.bookleafpub.com

E-mail: info@bookleafpub.com

ISBN: 9789358315158

First edition 2023

ACKNOWLEDGEMENT

Writing poems during one of the most difficult times in my life proved to be a major challenge. It wouldn't have been possible without my angel of a flatmate, and best friend, Catherine. She was with me every step of the way throughout these turbulent 21 days, supporting me in ways that only your closest friend can do. You will forever have a special place in my heart.

I'm eternally grateful to Mads, who - despite us not always communicating effectively with each other - did everything he could to be there for me, to support me in any way that I needed, and still continues to do so. You're a light in my life every time it goes too dark.

So much appreciation to my long-distance friend, Maja, who offered perspectives and love in a way that only she could do with deep insights into some of my feelings. We don't talk every day, but you're always in my thoughts.

Also a big thank you to my family. To my mum and dad, Pia and Finn, for offering to support me in any decision I made, proving that you'll always be there for me. To my sister, Michele, for being the first person to pick up the phone and speak to me when my whole world changed - and for offering your perspective and support. To my most amazing nephew, Emil, for always melting my heart and making me happy, even when I don't know how to find a smile.

A standing ovation and thank you to the friends who put up with me during these 21 days, supported me in the best way you could - stood by me and proved to be the most amazing people in my life. More specifically; Caroline, Katrine, Rebecca, Loredana, Gema, Luke and Máté.

Last, but not at all least, a big thank you to my therapist who jumped straight back into helping me out in her always professional and kind manner. I couldn't have gotten through it without your guidance.

A heartfelt thank you to all of you - I love you!

Thank You

My time with you was happy and I look back at
it with hope
Hope that there's a bright future for me where I'll
be happy again.
Again I can see there is light and you were my
"right now" guy
Guy with a strong mind and body, your hands
kept all stresses away
Away are some fears, and I found nature again
with it's peace
Peace was walking with you there, in our
comfortable silence
Silence in peace I'll miss the most - but I still
have a friend in you
You are an amazing human, who I loved and still
do.
Thank you

Doves

Happiness and love
The innocence of a dove
I'm happy above

Nightmares

At night I wake up screaming
My dreams and my mind aren't my own.
You invaded them with your actions
It's still here although I've grown.

I can clearly remember what you did
It's fresh like it happened today.
One day I'll have learned how to cope
So you'll no longer get it your way.

They're already fewer and further between
It's a fight I'll do all to win.
I'll say goodbye to all the things that you did
The world will be mine with a grin.

Freedom

I am so tired
Sickness is eating my mind
Freedom, in future

In My Room

I am alone, in my room, with my door closed
My insides hurt, whilst I'm crying my heart out
The feeling of loneliness; lingers

Sharing my feelings seems impossible
The old voice tells me that I can handle this on
my own
The feeling of being alone; lingers

I wish that I could turn off the demons inside my
head
Everyone is within reach to help, but I don't
reach out
The feeling of hopelessness; lingers

The Cough

The coughing, it hurts
Wondering, will death bring peace
But then - I'm cured

Goodbye My Blueberry

You were a surprise and I cried in panic
I already knew that this could only end tragic
In sorrow I told him and he reacted so well
But by then I was already under your spell

You are my blueberry and I'm filled up with love
You are growing within me, all snug like a glove
My mind still has demons, so I cannot keep you
But trust me when I say that is making me blue

Forever in my mind; you shall not be forgotten
Although there's a future that you will not be
brought in
Sadness fills me as I'm saying goodbye
But the decision is right, I'm not gonna lie

Goodbye my Blueberry

You Have No Power

There are days when I miss you and the man you used to be
 - the man who made me happy; you were truly good to me
But suddenly things happened and you decided to change
 - the good man was gone and it all became revenge
You started to control me and everything that I did
 - doing something wrong? Oh heaven forbid
Everything became hell and I felt so alone
- but hopefully one day you'll seek to atone
I finally left after you had broken me down
- it was that time I decided to leave our town
I lost friends on the way which was hard as all hell
- but the friends who still stayed kept wishing me well
New friends emerged; all these people became my path
- yet although they had me; in my head I still had your wrath
Family and friends have stuck by me, when I wanted to give up

- which thankfully means I'm slowly re-filling
my life's cup
There's still plenty of work to undo what you did
- and I am done hiding; opening up bit by bit
Good things are ahead and I'll reach my finest
hour
- you will have lost, as you no longer have the
power

Birthdays

Today I turned one year older.
I felt so alone - but boy was I wrong.
You all surprised me with an escape from my
sorrow.
You made me feel loved and seen.
My heart is bursting with the love I feel for you.
Thank you for making me feel whole.

Mirror

Mirrors and souls, tied
When I looked, tears and sadness
You helped; now? It's peace

See Right Through Me

From the first day I met you
I knew you were special
You made me feel safe
And you saw right through me

When you're in a room
All things bad go away
I feel free and relaxed
And you see right through me

When you're not here
I miss you and your scent
The troubles come back
And I wish you saw right through me

We'll never be together
Which truly makes me sad
But we'll forever stay friends
And you'll continue to see right through me

Peace

Laughter and smiles; you
Peace that it brings in my world
Dreams, they will come true

There's Hope

Sometimes life keeps throwing curveballs your
way,
Almost like you don't have a say.
You keep having to turn the other cheek,
Hoping that you're not too weak.

You're spending time proving to yourself that
you're strong,
So no more things can go wrong.
After some time you succeed,
Nothing else can compete.

Your insides start filling up with new hope,
There's now further strength to cope.
The future is bright,
You have won the fight.

Eyes

Oh those eyes you have
Every time I get lost in them
So deep, beautiful

Hold Me

In my tears,
You held me
In my sorrow you hold me tight.

In my pain,
You held me
In my darkness you hold me tight.

In my loneliness,
You held me
In my hopelessness you hold me tight.

In my hope,
You held me
In my happiness you hold me tight

There's Love There

I look into your eyes, and I see love in there
Love that you have for me, it's almost too much
for me to bear
The things you've experienced have broken you
Just like I've been ruined too.

Some days I have hope for the future, that our
love will find its way
But most days I'm filled with sadness, because
we have to keep it at bay
I hope you'll heal so you can be happy
Just like I want to be happy too.

You're Gone

The pain; the burning, pulsing and pressing pain.
So deep within it's almost unbearable.
I can feel you leaving my body and it's breaking
my heart.
Knowing that I'll never get to see you, never get
to feel you and never get to hold you.
Life will forever be changed, and although
you're now gone, you'll always be with me.
- My dear Blueberry.

Emptiness

My blueberry, gone
The emptiness, crippling me
Forgiveness, one day

www.ingramcontent.com/pod-product-compliance
Lightning Source LLC
LaVergne TN
LVHW041303200726
843507LV00014B/3113